The GENERATIONAL SAUCE

The
GENERATIONAL SAUCE

TWELVE VITAL
INGREDIENTS TO
OUTSHINE THE
COMPETITION

CHRISTOPHER MOTT

MOTTivation

www.MOTTivation.com

© Copyright 2024, Chris Mott

All rights reserved. This book or any portion thereof may not be reproduced or used in any manner whatsoever without the express written permission of the publisher except for the use of brief quotations in a book review.

Printed in the United States of America
First Printing, 2024

ISBN: 9798335105873

Imprint: Independently published

Cover Design & Creative Editing by: CreatiVerve
Print & eBook Productions by: CreatiVerve

Table of Contents

Chapter 1: Coincidence or Connection 7

Chapter 2: Knowing Your Audience 13

Chapter 3: Three Generational Truths 17

Chapter 4: You Hold the Keys 23

Chapter 5: Make it Automatic 25

Chapter 6: "I Know My Story" 29
    Ingredient #1

Chapter 7: I Champion Theirs 35
    Ingredient #2

Chapter 8: I Am Highly Relational 37
    Ingredient #3

Chapter 9: I Accentuate the Positive 43
    Ingredient #4

Chapter 10: I Fly High 49
    Ingredient #5

Chapter 11: I Forgive, and Forgive Again 53
    Ingredient #6

Chapter 12: I Am Present and Living in the Moment 57
    Ingredient #7

Chapter 13: I Am A Gentle Communicator 59
    Ingredient #8

Chapter 14: I Am Patient 63
    Ingredient #9

Chapter 15: I Am Grateful 69
    Ingredient #10

Chapter 16: I Find the Joy 71
    Ingredient #11

Chapter 17: I Love Big in Small Ways 75
    Ingredient #12

Chapter 18: Your Eulogy 83

Chapter 19: You Are the Secret Sauce 87

Chapter 1:
Coincidence or Connection

2023 started differently than any other. It was the aftermath of navigating my way through a pandemic. I suppose I didn't truly grasp how much the last two years' events could affect me. Perhaps I was naive and believed that I might be impervious to the changing energies of the universe. Maybe I was blinded to how much change, heartache, and suffering there was and how that might affect my psyche. After all, the entire planet had changed. Never before, at least in my lifetime, had we witnessed a whole planet falling to its knees at the hands of an invisible enemy. Never before have we seen millions of our fellow loved ones pass while suffocating above ground. Never before have I seen such division. We have been isolated in ways that are foreign to us. Perhaps I thought that I was exempt from loneliness. I was anything but immune. At the beginning of this year, I found myself uncertain. I found myself drained of self-confidence. I found myself down and lost.

Life changed, and it changed in significant, unpredictable, and unprecedented ways. As a result, I had to reinvent much of my professional existence. Pre-pandemic, I had a thriving speaking and coaching business. During the pandemic, much of that vanished. It was a full-on frontal attack on my identity. Please note: in the absence of identity, we find ourselves confused and seeking clarity. How did I react to this worldly shift? Well, my first plan was to eat and drink myself through it. That was a flawed plan at best. Why? Because the pandemic lasted way longer than my ill-conceived and unsustainable plan could maintain. After approximately a year of eating and drinking, all while watching my identity drift away, I decided to move in the direction of strength. This might sound super simple; the cure for weakness is strength.

When you feel compromised, do something that adds physical and mental value. Yes, it's that easy. Just change up the ingredients. Think about it. What's a bag of cement without the water? It's simply a bag of ingredients that possesses little to no integrity. However, when the water is added and the mixing process begins, it quickly forms a bond of strength, which is nearly impossible to separate. So, I responded by moving in a strong direction. I responded by adding an ingredient of strength. I responded by obtaining my Colorado Real Estate License and started selling residential real estate. It was indeed one of the best decisions. Why? Because it gave me purpose again. For most of my professional existence, there had been a desire to do it. But most important, it brought me back into relationships and community with people. It rejuvenated my soul. It was the true cure for what was ailing me. Fellowship was the cure for loneliness.

Anyone who knows me knows that I don't believe in coincidence. There's no such thing in my world. I know everything that happens, happens as a result of action or inaction. It occurs by the command of our weak or powerful thoughts. Those who believe in coincidence are merely the ones who fail to connect the dots. Everything, and I mean everything, if analyzed closely enough, is attached. That's precisely why your thoughts, words, and actions are so important. That trifecta is foreplay for your future.

With very pointed thoughts and specific actions, I plunged into real estate sales, and it took over. It filled the void that desperately needed to be filled. It gave me a new identity professionally. In doing so, it started to make me think. I was pondering not ever speaking in public again. I began to convince myself why I shouldn't do it anymore mentally. I mentioned the idea with my wife. Of course, when I did, it didn't go well. There was resistance. Not overbearing resistance, but rather, gentle pushback. Rachael said, "You shouldn't stop speaking. It's one of your gifts, and in doing so, you help thousands." Of course, she had to say that. She sleeps right next to me. It would be downright awkward and detrimental to our relationship if she were to tell me that I sucked as a motivational speaker. To compliment her sentiment, the universe decided to add its two cents. Have you ever received precisely what you needed from the universe at exactly the moment when you needed it? I bet this has happened numerous times. This is a prime example of connection rather than coincidence. I was moving energy around, but I was also conflicted. Conflicted is wishy-washy energy. It's indecisive. It's neither stop nor go.

I had questions, so the universe sent an answer in return. If you ask, you shall receive. The phone rang. Again, was it uncanny or perfect timing? It was perfect because I contemplated hanging up my flashy red jacket, which I always use for speaking engagements. It was perfect timing because it had been years since I'd received a call to speak. I recognized it as the universe sending a clear message. It was saying, "It's not time." I believe it was a message from God saying, we are not done with this pulpit quite yet. And so I said "yes."

There is great power in that one word, "yes." It signals to the universe that you're open and ready to receive opportunity and abundance. In my case, it opened up doors to a new speaking topic. I was chatting with the Coordinator of the event, which is called Market Trends. She said two amazing things during our call. One was they were excited to have me coming back. Yes, I had spoken for this conference in the past. Those words, when I needed affirmation, were food for my soul. They were so timely. Was it coincidence or connection? I believe it was connected. I was wishy-washy on my conviction, and the universe sent me affirmation in return.

Exactly what I needed and exactly when I needed it. But then she said the second thing, which would change the next three months of my life. She said, "Perhaps you could talk about what Gen Z wants." I replied immediately, "Absolutely, I can talk about Gen Z." Shortly after that statement, we ended the phone call, and I immediately asked myself, "What the hell is Gen Z!?" I get it. This is not my first rodeo. I know that sales professionals are always trying to analyze the current buying generation to discover the secret behind their purchasing motives. But I had been out of the game for some time and focused on other things. I was a little rusty on my current-day lingo. Looking back, I was led to discover a new topic and write this book entitled "The Generational Sauce." One sauce which is guaranteed to make anyone look irresistible in the eyes of any generation: 12 vital ingredients sure to make you stand out from the crowd. Do you understand the power of yes? Do you grasp the power of one opportunity? Are you ready to harness your true power? Get ready; it's all connected.

Chapter 2:
Knowing Your Audience

Anyone in sales will tell you that knowing your customer is essential. Back in the early 90's, I was new to the apartment management industry. I thought I knew it all. News flash! With age comes wisdom; in the absence of age and wisdom, all that remains is youth and enthusiasm. If we could discover a way to merge all of those characteristics, it would be a force. So early in my sales career, I had a lot of pent-up youthful energy and a ton of enthusiasm. I was lacking the wisdom to tie it all together. Before I was professionally trained in the art of sales, this pool of energy was released upon customers in what I now like to call "The Disneyland Tour." I would take prospective renters on community tours, and my presentation was downright automatic, so much so that no audience participation was necessary. Yup, back in the day, I thought I had it nailed. I thought I was the bomb when it came to sales. That delirious notion was shattered in the first few minutes of my first weeklong sales training course with the Oxford Management

Company. I had just landed a great position with the leader in property management and was ready to soak up everything they had to offer. That was until the Sales Trainer said, "Stop talking and start listening. It's the key to any successful sale." Hypocrisy! You just blew up my entire sales approach. Yes, I would go on sales tours and talk and talk. The problem was, I was giving too much info to my clients rather than very pointed information; which was what they really wanted. This was a reality check for sure. You shouldn't spend ten minutes talking about how great your Olympic-sized pool is, if your prospect doesn't know how to swim. I was making the tour process all about me when it needed to be about them. My mind was blown; there is always a better way.

This is it in a nutshell. Sales professionals must understand their customers. The Customer's wants and desires are crucial to designing a very pointed and on-target sales presentation. This is truly the key to building value. So, rather than just moving out on the sales tour, I began to slow my roll. I offered my clients a seat and was genuinely interested in their story or stories. What do I mean when I say story? It's simple. What road have you traveled thus far, and where are you headed now? That's your story. Why is story so important? Because people need to feel valued. When you take the time to get to know people, it changes the game. Why? Because individuals today are attention-deprived. And they're even more attention-deprived on the heels of social distancing and forced isolation. I'm not suggesting that you take advantage of weakness. That wouldn't be a solid or authentic energy. That would be the exact opposite. That would be an energy of going on the take rather than the give. That would be an energy your clients would indeed run from and mistrust. On the other hand, if you center and point your energy towards genuinely caring for others and loving each individual's story, you're sure to be welcomed with open arms.

It's super important to get to know people. I get it. But what frustrates me is our constant pursuit when it comes to figuring out what makes people tick. I get it. We are all different. We are a byproduct of our upbringing and it shapes our behavior. But in the same breath, I believe we are all the same. We are designed the same and created to be an individual masterpiece. I must admit. This constant pursuit to discover the secret to selling to a new generation makes my brain smoke. Yes, my mind and spirit are spinning in frustration. Why? Because having to constantly recreate the wheel is exhausting. There has to be just one way. One universal and consistent way to treat people. One that is sure to work for all generations. So, I headed down that path. I was in search of one way, the secret sauce.

Chapter 3:
Three Generational Truths

After those words were uttered, "Perhaps you could talk about what Gen Z wants?" I went into three months of intense study. Allow me to introduce you to Chris Mott. I am not a detail guy. I am a relationship guy. The other day, someone asked what kind of Jeep I owned. I replied with, "It's black." I said, "And my fishing pole is green, my raft is blue, my skis are yellow, and my wife is occasionally blonde." This is now a running joke regarding how I am built, but it's so true. I am just not a detail guy. I am not a consumer who researches something to the moon and back before I purchase. I think marketers purposely make things look shiny and exciting to specifically cater to guys like me who are just attracted to the next best thing. Can some of you relate? I believe this proves that we are all designed to be different and given distinct spiritual gifts. Take my business partner and myself, for instance. Our partnership is the epitome of iron sharpening iron. Matt is all about the details. He lives in a world of statistics and is a self-professed "data nerd." There is no other person who is more competent when it comes to market analytics. He is very black and white. He is also super talented, so I have nicknamed him "Scorsese." Why Scorsese? Because when it comes to film production, he is a savant. He completes me. But what he does makes me cringe. Why? Because what he excels in are my most significant challenges. On the other hand, he prefers not to deal with people, negotiate, or spend much time in relationships. That is where my strengths enter the picture. We are the perfect complement for each other. Together, we are a force.

This opportunity forced me to move outside of my comfort zone. I was forced to go deep. No more cliff notes or superficial Chris. The universe had a message for me but it was buried in the details. What was the message? It was that we were more the same than different. We need to stop labeling and paying attention to our perceived differences. The message and truth was that within all the generations, there are common threads. The common thread is the secret to appealing to everyone consistently. But before we go into the secret, we must discuss common threads. There are three, and I now call them "The three-generational truths."

Generational Truth #1 - Every generation believes the next generation is totally out of control. Ask them. Ask yourself. Have you ever thought that the world was coming to an end based on how far the next generation is pushing things? You have. Think about it. When Elvis came out on stage shaking his hips, all the young girls were fainting in the front row. It was an instant crush. Each one of them was head over heels in love or lust. In the same breath, all the parents were in the back row, fainting for a different reason. You see, back in the day, a young person wouldn't be permitted to go to a rock concert without a chaperone. Yes, the parents were fainting because they had just witnessed an unprecedented act by Elvis and his seductive moves. They thought the Devil was reincarnated. They felt that he was coming to take their children!

Every generation thinks that they are different than the one before it. Every previous generation thinks the next is anything but the same. A famous quote captures this notion to the "T." It goes like this.

> "The children now love luxury; they have bad manners, contempt for authority; they show disrespect for elders and love chatter in place of exercise. Children are now tyrants, not helpers, with their households. They no longer rise when elders enter the room. They contradict their parents, chatter before company, gobble up delicacies at the table, cross their legs, and control their teachers."

Sounds pretty relevant to what's happening with the current generation. Doesn't it? Do you know who wrote this and when? Socrates wrote it. Socrates lived from 469 to 399 BC. He lived when time was going backward. What point am I attempting to make? The generations have been pushing the limits from the beginning of time. It seems so different, but it's not. That's a common thread. Every generation is desperately searching for its own identity and pushing the boundaries of what's perceived to be acceptable. Again, a common thread. It's all the same, just in a different box. Why is this common thread worth paying attention to? Because if you know that others are just searching for their identity, then rather than condemning it, embrace it. Help them feel as though they matter and have a purpose. Help them feel worthy of belonging.

Generational Truth #2 - Every generation encounters tragedy and struggle. Again, each generation will try to proclaim that they have lived through the worst. You can hear them saying it; you know you can. "When we were young, we had to walk to school for miles. It was uphill both ways in the snow without any shoes!" It's all the same, no matter the competition, just packaged in a different box. World Wars, The Great Depression, Pearl Harbor, September 11th, Recessions, and the COVID-19 pandemic are all the same, but they seem different because they have unique labels. Their common denominator is that they all consist of tragedy and struggle. Why is it important to find the common thread within our struggles? Because we need to treat people with care, especially when they are struggling. It's essential to know how that tragedy is affecting them. It's called having empathy for the plight of others.

I always say, "I love a good tragedy." Is there such a thing as a good tragedy? Yes, I love tragedy with a caveat. I love tragedy as long as someone isn't getting hurt. Are you sick, Mr. Mott? No, I grasp the magnitude of the opportunity within any tragedy. Listen up, folks. When people are at their weakest, we can be at our strongest in how we respond and treat people during their time of need. It's beautiful and an opportunity to forge great loyalty when we step up in strength. Think about it. When a person is selfless and steps up to save one's life from a burning vehicle, the rescuer and the rescued forge an unbreakable bond. This is your chance to step into the hero role. This is your opportunity to save the day!

Generational Truth #3 - Our current struggle is made of the same detrimental disease. Have you ever studied about the life of Mother Teresa? If not, you should. She created a story of excellent results without a ton of resources. Think about Mother Teresa's brand. If you were asked to describe her in just a few words, what words would come to mind? Perhaps it would be selfless, giving, caring, impactful, and kind. The list is endless, but it's all cemented in a super-giving and robust frequency. Without a doubt, Mother Teresa created a brand cemented in eternity by her constant pursuit of her purpose. In researching her story, you will discover that she built a multinational organization with people who agreed to work long hours for no pay. These people were doing the worst of the worst jobs. Mother Teresa created this life-changing organization without a single dime from government funding. So the next time you choose to bark about a lack of resources, think back to Mother Teresa, and then think again about your plight.

When asked by a reporter to identify the most significant disease Mother Teresa had ever encountered, she answered with one word, "Loneliness." You would have thought she would have given a different answer. After all, she dealt with lepers, dying patients with aids, starvation, and the homeless, to name just a few. But out of all of them, she stated loneliness. Why? Because she could immediately treat the sick with medicine. She could comfort the dying. She could quench the thirst for food with nourishment. She could provide shelter to people experiencing homelessness. But to the lonely, it wasn't so easy. You see, loneliness is not the physical state of being alone. Instead, it's the perception that nobody cares. Here, we return to the power of story. News flash! You can be right with the right story or right with the wrong one. The choice is yours. I think the one to choose is a no-brainer.

Loneliness is not a joking matter. It's a belief cemented over time with no quick fix. It's super detrimental to the mind, body, and soul. The side effects of loneliness are known to be high blood pressure, heart disease, obesity, a weakened immune system, anxiety, depression, cognitive decline, Alzheimer's disease, and a lack of sleep. If that's not a recipe for an early grave, I don't know what is. Don't you find it ironic that in such a so-called connected society with five thousand Facebook friends, we are experiencing a loneliness epidemic? It makes perfect sense because most interactions with people are brief and superficial. They are anything but authentic and soul nourishing. This must change and change quickly. But what's the cure?

Chapter 4:
You Hold the Keys

As I travel around the country speaking, my regular audience is the Real Estate Industry. Why? Because my roots are there. Frankly, I can talk to anyone. If their hearts are beating, they are my audience. We have discovered that we are all the same while simply trying to live out our purpose amid universal struggles. Teaching this concept to the Real Estate Industry feels very relevant and on point. Why? Because those who assist others when it comes to creating a sense of home are also the ones who hold the keys to the cure for loneliness. What exactly is the cure? The cure is community. The cure is fellowship. The cure is a sense of belonging. The cure is a new and empowered story that goes like this, "People Care." Yes, it's that simple and powerful! Real estate professionals assist in finding or creating for their clients a sense of community. If they grasp the depth of their job description, they can bring fellowship and belonging to others. Therefore, they are the cure for loneliness; but only if they choose to grasp that powerful narrative and immense opportunity. In no way do I think that's exclusive to just the Real Estate Industry. I believe that opportunity is presenting itself to everyone.

So, a universal problem exists. Despite being more connected, we are lonelier than ever. I can see it. I hardly know all the neighbors on my street. Back in the day, as I was running around without shoes and playing in the mud, we knew everyone. This was the age of the block party. Remember those? Yes, the entire street would shut down, and all the neighbors would party in the street. We knew everyone. Why? Because that's just what you did. There was no Internet. There were no cell phones. So, naturally, we were coerced into being highly social with one another and thus lived in the warmth of community. These days, it's too easy to hide. It's too easy to cocoon. It's too easy to assemble the ingredients necessary to lead a lonely existence. I think it's high time that we grasp the key and embrace our true power. We hold the keys, and we have the cure. Step into community. Step into fellowship. Let's conquer this epidemic of loneliness together.

Chapter 5:
Make it Automatic

"Hurry, hurry, hurry." "Keep on pushing." "We need to keep pace with the competition." "We need to be on the cutting edge." These are all sayings that tax us beyond measure. I don't care what industry it is. This happens often. It seems as though the yearly mission is to shove as many new initiatives down the throats of our front-line team members. I get it; there is value in keeping up, maintaining your edge, and staying ahead of the competition. The problem is we are anything but balanced in our approach. Usually, it's balls to the wall and anything short of that is unacceptable. Balance is nowhere to be found, and our team members and customers suffer as a result. Why? Because balls to the wall condemns us to a constant state of change with little time to adapt. In this scenario, we are destined for mediocrity. Why? Because the adoption of actual change takes time. Impatience is anything but automatic.

The process of change is directly linked to behavioral change. Behavioral change is directly related to neuroscience. We all form habitual patterns over time. In layperson's terms, that means we all become accustomed to doing things in specific ways through repetition. To change these habits, it takes time, commitment, and reinforcement. The problem with Corporate America is they lack patience and the commitment to solidify lasting change. Corporate America is good at coming up with new ideas. They are good at pulling the trigger on new initiatives. But they are terrible when creating a safe and patient space, essential to solidifying lasting change. Why? Because they live in a delusional world where they believe they exist in a snap-your-fingers universe. Change never happens by snapping your fingers. Sorry, folks, it just doesn't work that way.

The other day, my wife approached me and asked, "Honey, can we move the garbage can in the kitchen?" I answered, "Where would you like it?" She said, "I don't care. I don't want it under the sink anymore as it's too cluttered." So, I had my marching orders. I went down to Wal-Mart and purchased the change: a stainless steel garbage can. I bought the change. I unpacked the change. And finally, I placed the change in the opposite corner of the kitchen. If only it were that simple. Do you know how long it took me to adjust my thinking/habitual behavior to the change? Six months! That's how long!

Why was it so difficult? Because there was a deep neural pathway that existed in my brain. It had been dug out and cemented in place over 55 years of repetitive training. I had been trained to throw the garbage out under the sink, and my mind wasn't buying a snap-your-fingers declaration of change. This process of change was both frustrating and humorous. Why was it frustrating? Because I couldn't grasp why my mind wouldn't switch over. I wasted time going to the kitchen sink and felt like an idiot. Why was it humorous? Because every time I habitually returned to the kitchen sink, my wife would gently make fun of me. As I returned to the garbage can, my wife would say, "Whatcha doing?" with a slight grin. As I shoved the garbage in my pants, I responded, "Oh, nothing, Honey. Just grabbing some cleaning products." She responded with. "You best get cleaning Buddy."

Epiphany Alert!

The older you are, the more time it takes to assimilate to change. The younger you are, the quicker the assimilation to change. No, this is not age discrimination. This is just science. This is just a fact. When we are young, our brains are simply more elastic. They adjust to change quicker. When we are older, our brains become more rigid. It's time to change that age-old saying to, "You can teach an old dog new tricks. You just need to be patient in doing so."

So what's the solution to the problem? How do we avoid becoming a functionally obsolete professional dinosaur while maintaining our competitive advantage? We need to identify specific areas of core excellence and protect and reinforce those areas with all our might. It's proven that doing one thing and one thing only in repetition leads to excellence. Take Michael Jordan, for instance. He was, without a doubt, if not the greatest basketball player, at the very least, one of the greatest. With three seconds left on the game clock and trailing by just two points, the head coach of the Chicago Bulls would call a timeout. The team would huddle around to draw up their final play. It didn't take a rocket scientist to figure out what they would do. The ball was always going to be in Jordan's hands. It didn't matter who was covering him. It didn't even matter how many were surrounding him. He would drop back a foot from coverage, take the jump shot, and, without a doubt, hit a game winning three-pointer. How was Michael so consistent? Because he simplified the process. He never tried to reinvent himself. It was always about doing one thing and one thing well. It was all about scoring. It has been said that one summer, Michael shot six thousand practice shots per week for the entire summer. With practice comes perfection. We were constantly amazed at his excellence when the game was on the line, but we shouldn't have been. It wasn't about that one shot but all the shots before it. Think about my garbage can analogy. I was on autopilot when it came to throwing away the garbage. Michael became automatic with a basketball, and his garbage can was a hoop.

You may need a more down-to-earth example. If so, take a look at the food truck industry. The industry has transformed as of late and is now wildly popular. What was once known as the "roach coach" has become an industry of super niche high-end eateries. They are not known for a wide selection of items, as there's no room to stock the inventory to support such variety. So, they simplified their menu and started producing a limited amount of specialties to delight customers. They became automatic and, in turn, became wildly successful.

So, the moral of the story is this. Don't keep changing for the sake of changing. Stick with what you do best and make it automatic. Find your secret sauce, one recipe for success, and stick to it. My sauce, which I have discovered within five-plus decades, consists of 12 vital ingredients and they are as follows.

Chapter 6:
"I Know My Story"

Ingredient #1

Think about that statement. "I know my story." It sounds pretty definitive. If it sounds rock solid, that's intentional. Why? Because I am a Life Coach. Every day, I teach others to write powerful stories for themselves. I teach them to declare their intentions in the here and now. While coaching others, I often find individuals writing with a weak frequency. Clients tend to push their desired goals and accomplishments down the road. They write statements such as "I will know my story." Notice how different that sounds from "I know my story." The energy between the two statements is drastically different. One claims it in the here and now, and the other places its fruition down an indefinite road. If we desire to accomplish or become something, we must claim it in the here and now. If we do the opposite, we kick the can down the road, and there's no telling where it will eventually land. It's nebulous. If your wish is to be, then you must declare it to be.

There are two pens when it comes to the stories that we adopt. There is our pen, the stories that we write for ourselves. Then there is the pen that others hold for us. That pen is made up of how people perceive us. Allow me to bless you with a real-life story written by someone else for me. Earlier this year, as I mentioned at the beginning of this book, I encountered one of the most challenging months of my life, minus of course the months after my parent's deaths and excluding the months after my divorce from my first wife. A substantial contributing factor to my struggle was that I adopted a story written about me by someone else.

Here's some back-story so you're armed with some context. Earlier this year, I was working with a client of ours. I could tell that the relationship between this client and myself was not "clicking" like all the rest. I take great pride and derive significant satisfaction from the click. But I am here to tell you. You're not designed to click with everyone. So, amid this transaction, I had gone to California for some much-needed family time, and when I returned, my business partner approached me. He said, "I need to have a conversation with you, and I am not looking forward to it." I replied, "Stop right there; I know what it is. Let me guess. The client does not want to work with me and would rather work with you." My business partner's face was mystified. "How did you know that?" He asked. I replied with, "Dude, this is not my first rodeo. I'm a relationship guy. I know when the energy is off." But then he said something that cut. The client said, "I find no value in Chris." Ouch! That hurt! I played it off that it didn't, but it did. My business partner even called attention to it. He was pushing back on my deflection and cavalier attitude, as he knew my primary love language: words of affirmation. He was right. But I wouldn't admit to the comment's fullest extent of soulful carnage. Perhaps it was because I didn't realize how much it would affect me. News flash! Hurtful words said by others are like termites attacking our vitality. If left unchecked, they are destined to do significant damage. I blew these off, and I should have known better. I allowed the termites in, and they raked havoc in my life. I mean, it was terrible. I was looking around, mystified and asking myself what was wrong. I was downright depressed and, at the peak of my despair, was considering seeing a psychiatrist as I thought that perhaps the chemicals in my body had gone awry.

As I was unpacking this story with the circle of trust surrounding me, family, friends, and trusted mentors, I stumbled upon something that may stick with me for the rest of my existence. Besides cutting me with the worst knife possible, words, I discovered my greatest fear. What if I were to get to the point of adding no professional value? My greatest fear is adding no value at all. That was it! Revelation! He struck at my Achilles heel. But here lies the most significant lesson in it all. I gave someone the power that didn't warrant the power. I allowed someone who knew nothing of me and my soul to have more weight than they deserved. That's the lesson. If you choose to listen to others, listen to those who matter the most in your world.

Now for an example of my mighty pen... I need to transport you back to March of 2016. What happened in March of 2016? I enjoyed engaging in a two-day process facilitated by my wife, Rachael. Rachael is a certified Life Planner from the Patterson Group in Boulder, Colorado. Life Planning is a process where the facilitator circles your life for two days to discover your journey's ups, downs, and trends. Without a doubt, it's both an exhausting and revealing process. One of the exercises near the end of the process is to write your purpose statement. My purpose statement was...

> "I am a Life Sherpa who sprinkles others with strength and balance to unveil their true masterpiece."

It's pretty solid and unique, right? Those who know me personally and those who know my book, "Find Your Sprinkles," know this is totally on target. I didn't grasp how powerful this purpose statement would be when I wrote it. Fast forward to 2021. We are in the throes of the COVID-19 pandemic, and my speaking income has evaporated because we are not meeting in public anymore. Much of my coaching income has dried up, as most can't afford coaching. I was coaching more, just not for compensation. Why? Because God gave me the gift to coach. I didn't do anything to deserve it; so blessing it forward, as He did with me, is fitting. So it's all gone, all the income is gone, so as mentioned, I transitioned into Real Estate sales. While courting numerous Brokerages in my hometown, I stumbled upon Sherpa Real Estate. Rachael and I invited the owners of Sherpa over for dinner. Their names were Chris and Rachel as well. After speaking to Chris briefly, I discovered his mother's name was Phyllis, just like my Mom.

Coincidence or connection? God was trying to hammer this one home. He was clearly saying that this was where I was destined to be. Have you ever had that happen? The signs are plentiful and so straightforward that it feels like The Almighty is trying to hit you with a Mack truck. Yes, this was one of those times. As we were sitting around a campfire chatting, my wife Rachael jumped up and ran into the house. She returned with my life planning book from five years previous and said, "Do you realize what you wrote!? You wrote that you were a Sherpa, and now you must be a Sherpa!" So much for my leverage in negotiation. Thanks, Honey. I had no choice but to sign on the dotted line; the feeling was mutual. Do you now understand the power of story? Do you know that the power of adopting stories into your existence can go both ways? They can crater you if they are weak and inspire and fuel you if they are strong. Either way, they are sure to affect your present and future. There's only one option. Grab the mighty pen and only adopt stories worthy of your masterpiece.

Chapter 7:
I Champion Theirs

Ingredient #2

Have you ever noticed what people do when they're accepting an award? They always thank the people who helped them get there. They ooze with gratitude for others and want to celebrate those who championed their story. Rita Pierson is a lifelong educator. She delivered a super popular Ted Talk. It's a must-watch if you get the chance. I always say that my two favorite types of people are teachers and nurses. Why? Because in my mind, they are the ultimate caregivers. They care for the weak and promote strength. There is just something about a caregiver's energy that is super attractive.

If you want to spend seven minutes of your time wisely, then look up Rita on YouTube. What a great speech regarding the genuine opportunity when it comes to championing the stories of others.

She delivered many excellent points during her TED talk, but the following stood out most. She stated human connection is vital, and kids don't learn from those whom they don't like. I don't believe these points are exclusive to just the classroom. I don't think these nuggets of wisdom are exclusive to just the young. I think they apply to life in general and are multi-generational. Yes, we are designed to live in community with one another. Human connection is vital. No, it's not something that can be obtained via the Internet. True connection must happen in person. We need to touch people via their souls; showing up is the best way to accomplish that.

Here's the truth. We are super receptive to others and their opinions when we like the person. Strike that. Let's change the word like to love. When we love them, it's for a reason. It's because they care and are more than willing to champion our story. The bottom line is this. You will go to the mat for someone you love. Love someone else's story, and they will love you in return. But here's the kicker. It would be best if you championed the personal and professional story, preferably the personal first and foremost.

How does one Champion the story of another? Remember the story of my Disneyland tour? It was a story of caring little about the person across from me. Championing someone's story is precisely the opposite. To support the story of another, you need to know everything and anything about the person in question. It takes time. It takes an authentic and inquisitive nature. It's achieved by sincerely caring about discovering one's past, present, and future. Once you find out the road they have traveled, it's sure to provide you with the key to unlock the full potential of their glorious story. Once you can see the finish line, it's super easy to champion their story to fruition.

Chapter 8:
I Am Highly Relational

Ingredient #3

Do you know which people in the workplace are the loneliest? Haven't you ever heard that expression? "It's lonely at the top." Well, it's true. A Harvard study indicates that over half of CEOs feel lonely. It reports that sixty-one percent say it impedes their work performance. News flash! Of course, it does, as loneliness is an all-out attack on your mind, body, and soul. We have already mentioned all the adverse health effects linked to loneliness. This is a perfect recipe for giving less. Why? Because if you desire to provide more, you must possess more first.

Loneliness within Leadership is mainly self-inflicted. How can that be? It happens because many Leaders lead via deficient narratives. Why? Because they were never trained to be strong Leaders. They were never blessed with a strong story to guide them. More often than not, Leaders are promoted into a position of responsibility due to some above-average production. Therefore, they are instantly dubbed a Leader. The problem is that leadership takes a whole different skill set than what led them there. Leaders must have a mission and supporting narratives that reinforce that mission. This is where I will raise my hand. Why? Because early in my leadership career, I was one of those Leaders who led with some weak underlying narratives and created some self-inflicted loneliness. What does a self-defeating leadership narrative look and sound like? Here's an example.

> *"I don't get too close to my employees because I don't want it to affect my ability to discipline or fire them if need be."*

Yup, that was me. I had and led by that narrative. You know how they always say hindsight is twenty-twenty? It is so true. Looking back at this flawed narrative, I now see it was absolute craziness. We have already demonstrated how powerful our stories are when manifesting strength or weakness. Diagnose and take a hard look at how damaging this story is. First off, "employees" is such a vanilla and sterile word. These are people. They are souls! When we sterilize things, it's super easy to treat them with little to no care and or respect. Souls deserve our care and admiration for the opportunity that each one represents. In that same sentence, I wrote phrases like "too close" and negative words like "discipline" and "fire." Why do I find this statement to be half-cocked at best?

Because what you lead with is sure to follow. I wrote this way before I became a Life Coach. This statement promotes weakness and struggle. It leads to division. Think back to what Rita Pierson taught us. For someone to learn from another, they need to be highly connected and love the person instructing them. Does division and negativity seem like a good recipe for connection and love? I think not! Why would you lead with a detrimental result if you knew your leading energy must come to fruition? Why would you lead with a damaging result in mind if your goal was the opposite? Ignorance is the answer. I was downright oblivious.

It's popular these days for individuals to claim that they must set healthy boundaries. I don't buy it. I am calling BS. Why? Because I think the word "boundaries" is a clever disguise for division. I don't believe boundaries are necessary when acting or leading in strong and ethical ways. I know it's taboo or perhaps not so "PC" to mention the word love in the workplace, but it's essential. "I love the job that you're doing." "I love having you as part of our professional family." I love working with you." All these phrases are perfectly acceptable unless they are said with unacceptable undertones. Said with love, honesty, and respect, they can never be misinterpreted. They are what others need to hear. Why? Because everyone wants to be loved. Again, kids don't learn from those whom they don't like and love. Whether team members or clients, people do not stay unless they are loved. It's that simple.

So what's the solution? No walls. No division. You must walk through life with people and create a sense of connection. Allow me to give you an example of when I struggled with a lack of connection and an overabundance of division. Back in the day, when I was the Director of Property Management for a Real Estate Development firm in the Silicon Valley of California, I was having some conflict with an Accountant who also worked at the same company. We didn't see eye to eye. She was very black and white, and I floated around in the clouds. I was very flexible, and she was the exact opposite.

We were the epitome of oil and water. One day, my frustration eventually came to a head, and I marched into the Owner of the firm's office and said, "It's either her or me, but someone must go!" I had reached my breaking point! The Owner of the company paused and asked me a straightforward question. He said, "Chris, are you traveling to Utah next week?" I replied, "Yes, but what does that have to do with my problem?" He replied, "I want you to take her to Utah with you." I think I either fainted mentally or went into an uncontrollable seizure at the thought of his direction. If I board a plane with this Gal, I might be tempted to open the hatch and push her out! He said, "I am not asking; I'm telling." I guess he put me in my place. So off we went to Utah.

I had to sit with her in the airport, sit next to her on a plane, travel around with her, and, more importantly, break bread with her for two days, three meals a day. Did we return from Utah as best friends? No, we did not. But did I return with a greater understanding of who she was and what she was going through? Absolutely! Over our travels, we were forced to make small talk and develop a closer relationship. I found out that she was a mother of three teenagers. That alone would be enough to make anyone a bit crazy, as teenagers are the most heinous creatures on the planet. I also discovered that she was divorced, and that her ex-husband was terribly abusive.

She struggled to make ends meet financially, so her job and being good at what she did professionally was essential. And I wanted her fired! Shame on you Chris Mott! That's like kicking an old guy after falling in the park. I hate to admit it, but the Owner's suggestion was brilliant. He was a very crafty Leader. He realized that there was not a lot of connection between us. He knew the connection was missing, as was understanding and empathy. Here's the ultimate lesson. People who exist in relationship, very rarely live in lasting conflict. People who exist in relationship, are more apt to extend grace towards one another. People in deep relationship, are more prone to feeling connected and are rarely lonely. Go out and be highly relational.

Chapter 9:
I Accentuate the Positive

Ingredient #4

D o you know how often clients proclaim that they are positive in coaching? It happens all the time. And then, I give them a writing assignment, and not a single positive word hits the paper. Yes, we often live in a delusional world regarding our perception of ourselves. We often think our poop doesn't stink, but oh, does it reek! Wake up and smell the coffee, folks. By nature or due to behavioral conditioning, we are very negative creatures.

Fact check alert! I am still determining where the following statistics came from, but I have been quoting and preaching about them for decades. Just for practicality's sake, let's assume they are true. It's been said that every human has, on average, 30 thousand thoughts daily. Of those thoughts, 85 percent are inherently negative. And of the thoughts that pop into your head today, 95 percent of them are a plagiarism of yesterday's thoughts. Now that, if you believe in the law of attraction, is a terrible batch of statistics. Why? Because it implies we are on the proverbial hamster wheel of negativity and can't get off. The problem is that if the old saying holds, "We reap what we sew," we are in deep trouble. Why? Because we are sewing the seeds of negativity by the thousands daily. We're destined to manifest more negativity if we don't bail off this hamster wheel. It's high time to jump off that dysfunctional and detrimental wheel.

Often, it's sneaky. We slide into negativity without an ounce of awareness. Take couples, for instance. Quietly observe the dialogue of couples that have been together for some time. Why am I using this as an example? Because I coach couples constantly. There is a common occurrence that happens between them. They start to correct each other not occasionally but often. One will tell a story and reference something such as "We met a friend at 2 p.m." And before the person telling the story even pauses, the spouse chimes in with, "No, it was 1 p.m." Who cares about the discrepancy? This frankly drives me bonkers. Why have you drifted into the mode of having to pick out every little flaw? If this trait between couples drives me crazy, imagine what it does to the person being critiqued. Think about how far you have fallen. At the beginning of your relationship, the person across from you couldn't say or do anything wrong. And now it's all wrong. How attractive is that? It's not, and it's a perfect recipe for divorce. No, not the kind of divorce that is exclusive to just marriage. I'm talking about relational divorce. Nobody wants to be around negativity. Nobody wants to be around someone who constantly picks out their flaws. Life changer alert! You can't ever be right in a relationship by making the other person feel wrong. When you create a win-loss scenario, you both lose.

Do you want to read a great book on this subject? Don't worry. It's a super quick read for all you nonreaders out there. It's only six chapters entitled Whale Done, written by Ken Blanchard. Be forewarned. It was written back in the day when we all carried around pagers like drug dealers. Do you remember those days? We would call back random numbers without question. How crazy does that sound? These days, if a random number pops up, it's destined for voicemail. We aren't answering a random number as we are too busy for that nonsense. Oh, have times changed. Yes, it was written back in the day of pagers and when it was perfectly acceptable to catch a killer whale and put it in a goldfish bowl to delight human beings. Again, not to "PC" anymore. In my coaching practice, I give this book out often to clients to read. After doing so with one client, she immediately messaged me back and said she couldn't get through the book because she was too distraught about the whales' captivity. I appreciated this client's sensitivity but encouraged her to push forward and finish it to receive the overarching message. I also reminded her that we have already freed Willy, so the story has an ultimate happy ending.

I was one of those guys. I was living in a delusional state and thinking that I was a super positive spirit. But in reality, back in the days of my property management career, I acted out in all kinds of ways contrary to accentuating the positive. I remember listening to Whale Done as my wife and I were traversing the country on one of our many road trips. There are just times when you're supposed to receive a message. This was, without a doubt, one of those times. This book was a huge wake-up call. "Wake up, you big Buffoon!" On this day, the universe held up the mirror to expose my delusional hypocrisy. It worked. I immediately realized that I was feeding an insatiable desire for attention on behalf of my audience but in the wrong way.

What exactly was I doing? I was a master of pointing out the flaws. I was eagle-eyed when it came to picking out the negative. I would visit properties and terrorize people. It was never intentional. Words of caution, often when we are carelessly unintentional, it can lead to a state of anything but connection. I would make lists of everything that was deficient and demand the correction. How was this positive? Perversely, I thought it was. I thought it was the means to perfection, so it had to be positive. Wrong! All it was, was igniting the law of attraction in a direction contrary to my desire. Again, remember, what you lead with is sure to follow. Accentuate the negative, and you're destined to receive more in return. What a buffoon!

The book Whale Done draws attention to the whale's attention-deprived state in captivity. Sound familiar? After the recent pandemic, it sure does. I don't know about you, but I am a hugger, and after two to three years of minor to no hugging, I am downright hug-deprived. I have some significant ground to make up! So if you see me on the street, watch out! Get anywhere close, and a hug is sure to come your way. My apologies. I digress. Back to the whales and the fact that they are attention-deprived. Back to the law of attraction. Do you know what incarcerated attention-deprived creatures yearn for the most? Attention. And here may be the most profound point of this chapter. Attention-deprived creatures don't care what kind of attention they receive just as long as they are receiving it. It does not matter if the attention is positive or negative. They are so thirsty for attention that they will take it any way they can. Therefore, if rewarded negatively for negative behavior, they will do more of the same. Think about this practically. Raising your voice to your child because they stepped out of line is a reward. You might as well say, "Keep acting out negatively because I like it." I know. It's not what you want, but that is the message you send with misguided attention.

If you accentuate the negative with people, you will feed their desire for attention, but in a losing way. People are conditioned to do more of the same, especially if you reward them. Logically, from a negative standpoint, it doesn't make sense. But when it comes to behavioral science, it makes perfect sense. People will take attention any way they can get it. So, the moral of the story is this. If you want more positive results, you must seek out people doing good and reward them with your attention. You must catch them in the act of good.

My ultimate takeaway from Whale Done is the following. If I were ever to return to my old career, I would change things significantly. I would accentuate the positive rather than visiting sites and calling attention to the negative. I would suppress the micro-manager in me who needed to point out every little flaw, and I would find everything that people were doing correctly. I would celebrate the positive. I would then challenge them to find ten more ways that they can even be better by my next visit. Think about this. Who would you rather work for? The person who is constantly pointing out all your flaws or the person who is celebrating your masterpiece? The answer is a no-brainer.

Chapter 10:
I Fly High

Ingredient #5

Have you ever woke up in a perfect mood, and then the day took a negative turn? It seemed like everywhere you turned, life was trying to knock you off your lofty position of positivity. If so, you are not alone. This happens all the time. This is where we should clarify the similarities or differences in our belief set. In my world, this occurrence, when life is trying to knock you down a peg, is known as spiritual warfare. I believe in God and Satan and that Satan is constantly attacking through people and circumstances to rock us from our Godly perch. Perhaps you don't believe what I believe.

Contrary to popular belief, that is perfectly ok. Just because we don't think the same way or believe the same things doesn't mean that one of us is terrible and the other is good. We humans are too quick to declare what's good and evil. We don't allow things to play out and are premature to issue a verdict. How many times have you done this? How often have you declared something to be terrible and had to eat crow because some force turned it into good? I bet it happens more often than not; unless you are just viewing the world through a prism of negativity. To me, that rebound force is God working in every situation to create good. Regardless of your belief, you have noticed some force trying to knock you down. You have also experienced another force trying to boost you up. The fact is, even in our perceived differences, we have things in common. We all struggle with the same things. They may look different, but it's still a struggle.

Now that we have discovered that we are equally yoked in our struggle, allow me to tell you a story about living in Colorado. Colorado is, without a doubt, one of the most beautiful places on the planet. When we decided to move here from California, my only request to my wife was that we be on some kind of water. There I go again, writing a powerful story for myself, and the story coming true. We now live on the San Juan River in Pagosa Springs and we not only own one river home, but two. Be careful what you wish for, as your dreams are bound to come true. When we eventually found a place to call home, we bought it lock, stock, and barrel. We lived a minimalistic existence then, having traveled around in our Airstream trailer for approximately two years. Yes, we went from having very little in a hot second, to having a ton. The reason being, we had negotiated to buy our home fully furnished. We purchased silverware, dishes, linens, knickknacks, snow blowers, lawnmowers, snowmobiles, and one white water raft. I remember Rachael looking at the raft and asking, "So, what do you know about that raft?" I replied, "It's blue, and has paddles." Rachael responded, "Those are not paddles; those are oars, and you are going to rafting certification school." So there she went; she booked me into ten days of extensive river training during the peak of winter snow melt, and she went to warm, sunny Florida and sunk her feet in the sand. I remember receiving pictures from her of Mai Tai's on the beach while I was in full splash gear as it was sleeting, raining, snowing, and thundering simultaneously.

I remember the first training day and how they explained all the ways you could die on the river! I thought my wife loved me!? Perhaps she was trying to "off" me? All kidding aside, Rachael was right. She is always right. She knew the river could be deadly if we didn't know what we were doing. When a good friend of mine discovered we were moving to Colorado, he said, "Chris, just remember, you can end up on the wrong side of Colorado quickly, so be prepared for everything." They were both right, and one of the most excellent rafting and life lessons I learned during my ten-day certification was dealing with the unexpected. They taught us that the river will throw the unexpected at you. How true is this in life? It happens all the time. But when it does, there is just one cardinal rule. The cardinal rule is this. The Captain can never say, "Oh crap!" Why? Because it makes the rest of the people in the boat very nervous. Now that is sage life advice.

We must know our job description at all times. We must know how to carry ourselves. We must be ready for the unforeseen obstacles and challenges that lie waiting for us around each and every corner. And when we encounter them, it's not our place to lower ourselves into the moment's energy. It's our job to continue to fly high above the fray. As a young parent, I didn't always fly high.

Nothing used to push my button more than little children melting down. If I could go back and do it differently, I would. I would do it with much more patience, discipline, and restraint. As a newbie parent, I was a screamer. Not my finest moment in life. I would scream at my children to calm down as they looked at me like I had three heads. You're telling us to calm down while you're losing your collective crap? That's rich. Ok, pot kettle, get it together, Dad. Yes, I was emotionally immature back then. I was often just a pawn in the game of dysfunctional energy. I would be easily coaxed into a lower position, and because of it, my life was anything but peaceful. Here in lies the lesson. When others are on the crazy train, it's not your job to join them. It's your job to use your words, actions, and demeanor to slow the train down gently. Fly high. You're sure to be respected for it.

Chapter 11:
I Forgive, and Forgive Again

Ingredient #6

Keep no record of wrongs. Easier said than done. We are like walking filing cabinets with document after document and file after file of all the transgressions around us. You've heard them say it. "You always do this." That statement is a clear indication of someone keeping a mental list. It's also a gross exaggeration. I haven't met a single person who is consistent and disciplined enough to claim the title of "always." Why is it so important not to keep a record? Because what we hold onto, we are sure to manifest more of in our future. So what's the answer? If I'm not keeping a record, then what's the alternative? It's forgiveness. It's wiping and keeping the slate clean.

But there must be a limit to my forgiveness. I can't be a doormat and let people run all over me. News flash! Forgiveness is not a sign of weakness; it's a sign of great discernment, discipline, and strength. When I was first divorced, there was not enough forgiveness to be found. In its absence, there was just anger. There was hatred, and God wasn't anywhere to be found. Of course, He was there. He is always there. But I didn't recognize Him as my vision was clouded by anything but strength. I was the farthest thing from free. I had incarcerated myself by stepping into a weak, rather than strong, energy. Think about that for a bit. Yes, was I hurt by others? Most certainly, I was. But after a period of transgression, it was all on me. It was my choice to carry the story and the compromised energy forward. Oh, and did I. I was the poster child for the victim. I was like a walking file cabinet of crap; my drawers were wide open. My misery was on full display. So the question is, who's the worst offender? Is it the person who does it first, or is it you who does it to yourself repeatedly from that point forward? I think the answer is simple: it's the repeat offender.

What is forgiveness? Well, I will tell you what it isn't. It's not forgiving but not forgetting. Forgiveness is one hundred percent, or it's not even close. Forgiveness is understanding and empathy. Forgiveness is emotional and spiritual maturity on full display. Why understanding? Because you need to know where the transgression is coming from in the first place. The flesh is never our enemy. Dark forces work to exploit the weaknesses in others. They do so to cause conflict. They do so to sew the seeds of division. If they trick you into blaming someone, they win, and both of you lose. Forgiveness is the wisdom to identify the true culprit. It's understanding that a person can be compromised and having the grace not to assign blame to that person. Why is there no assignment of blame? Because the assignment of blame always places you in the victim's position and diminishes others.

Imagine going on a job interview and saying, "Hire me. I am going to keep a record of everyone. Yes, that's right! I am keeping a record of all the negatives!" How attractive would you be? Can you say, "Absolute nut job?" Or perhaps "Bat dung crazy!" Yes, that would sum it up. There's not even the slightest chance you are getting that job. Can you imagine going on a date and telling the person across from you that you can remember every bad thing your X did to you? Check, please! That's the end of that date. Ask yourself. Am I collecting the transgressions of others? If so, am I championing the story of that person? That's the exact opposite of being a champion. Perhaps a negative one. This will undoubtedly lead in one direction and one direction only, the direction of division. Forgive and forgive again. Why? Because it's attractive.

Chapter 12:
I Am Present and Living in the Moment

Ingredient #7

Are you one of those who warmly asks someone how they are but do not want to hear the answer? "Nope, can't stop right now. Tell me later." That's not cordial. That's superficial. Or perhaps you rush through the grocery store to arrive at the checkout lines and get stopped. You immediately size up each line. You start to calculate logarithms in your head. You add up the amount of items in each cart. You times that number by the carts in front of you and then divide that number by the age of the Checker. If you are laughing hysterically right now, it's because it's you. This is so you! You are that person! And it doesn't stop there. Once you're in line, you are anything but calm. You are competitive! You constantly look at the other lines to see if you made the right decision. You start coaching the Checker and the Bag Boy if the race is close between your line and the one next to you. "C'mon, Checker, you are a scanning machine! You can do this! Faster! Faster!" "Let's go, Bag Boy! Assume the catcher's position, as these items are coming in hot! This is what legends are made of, and this is your time to shine!" And when you are finally victorious, you're high-fiving everyone and strutting your stuff around the grocery store. If a referee were present, you most assuredly would be flagged for taunting. Yes, you may have won the checkout race, but you are losing at the game of life. Why? Because you are being anything but present and living in the moment. I must give credit where credit is due. I heard this jovial scenario from Doug Fields during a sermon at Mariners Church in Irvine, California. If you have never heard Doug speak, put it on your bucket list. If you have never read one of Doug's many books on parenting or marriage, they are game changers.

Let me spell it out if you haven't drawn the correlation yet. All twelve ingredients are vital for The Generational Sauce, but certain unique ingredients genuinely are the cure for what ails us. Being present and living in the moment with others is one of those vital ingredients. Take yourself back to the chapter on Mother Teresa. What did she say? She said that the worst disease that she had ever encountered was loneliness. And again, what is loneliness? It's the perception that nobody cares. If you become consumed by being busy to the point that you have no time for others, you have become the problem. So the operative question is, "Do you wish to be part of the problem or the solution?" Remember this. Our actions speak louder than words. If you choose not to spend time with people, you can exacerbate their weak narrative regarding loneliness. Grasp this. Busy is the enemy of an abundant life that is grounded in relationships.

Chapter 13:
I Am A Gentle Communicator

Ingredient #8

One of the most valuable books I've ever read about building solid relationships is The Five Love Languages. The author is Gary Chapman, and it will take you 5 to 10 minutes to go online and take the test to obtain your primary two love languages. Or are you just too busy? Perhaps you are too busy to be bothered by love and relationships. Are you noticing a consistent theme yet? Yes, it's all weaving itself together.

I won't be getting into all the five love languages in this book, but I recommend that you study them all. You will find that all of them are essential when connecting with others. This book was a true game changer for me, and I now teach its principles to my coaching clients all the time. However, it wasn't until years after my first experience with the book that I understood how love languages could move in two different directions. What do I mean exactly? I mean, you can both love and deeply hurt others via their love languages. Allow me to offer you a real-life example. My two primary love languages are "words of affirmation" and "physical touch." My wife's primary two love languages are 'gifts of service" and "quality time." As we know, women love to give men what they call "The honey do list." Wake up and pay attention! The honey do list is just a clever disguise for an opportunity to love someone via gifts of service. By nature, whether you want to admit it or not, we are all selfish beings. When I am being selfish, it's my nature to operate on autopilot within my two primary love languages. I walk around saying nice things and physically touching my wife. When I do so, I assume she must feel like the most loved woman on the planet. Wrong! For her to genuinely feel loved in the most effective way possible, I must step out of my love languages and into hers. Why was I missing the mark in this area? Because it was easy for me to be selfish. It was automatic. It was my nature. It becomes much more complicated when someone you care about has the opposite love languages than yourself. Why is it challenging? Because it takes vigilance and effort to step out of your autopilot and into the love languages of others.

My wake-up call came when I realized the worst thing I could ever do was to put my wife's love languages down the priority totem pole lower than my own. If I intended to hurt her, that would be the best way. Again, remember what loneliness is. "A perception that people don't care." Why would I ever want to exacerbate a feeling of loneliness within one of the people I care for the most? I wouldn't. But when I am consumed by busyness, it's super easy to create unintentional collateral damage. Often, when we hurt others, it's accidental. Then, there are highly intentional times. No matter the circumstance, they are both equally detrimental.

Be gentle in all of your ways. When gentle is nowhere to be found, our communication style is often careless. Frankly, most of us have become terrible communicators. We are texting, emailing, and taking the easy way out for expedience, and those around us suffer. Face it. We are too busy to communicate effectively. Here's a life lesson. It doesn't mean you should use it just because it's at your disposal. Cell phones are not helping us when it comes to being effective communicators. As I always tell my clients, "Texting is for love and logistics only." If you would like to text me that you love me, that's fantastic. If you need to coordinate a pick-up on 4th and Main at 4 p.m., then that's perfectly acceptable. But if you have anything of weight or measure to chat about with anyone, you best do it in person. Why? Because they deserve your presence. They deserve to hear how you feel in the flesh. They deserve your respect and actions, which reinforce that notion. Text is the worst vehicle for dealing with essential topics because people can't feel your energy. Without feeling, others are free to write a story about what they believe you are thinking and feeling. What have we learned about the kinds of stories that people usually write? They are almost always negative. Why is being a gentle and thoughtful communicator vital to the Generational Sauce? Because the absence of care and vigilance when it comes to using your words is the devil's playground. I wish it were easy. I wish it came as second nature. But when we couple the weapon of the word with a careless and irresponsible demeanor, it's sure to head in the wrong direction.

Why is being gentle so important? Because people are keeping a record. We're encouraged not to keep a record of every wrong, but we do. We are like walking filing cabinets when it comes to the transgressions of others. We have already discussed this. We've stated that we need to forgive and forgive again. We may do so, but we often fail to forget. Yes, we must do that as well. Why? Because the occurrences which we fail to forget, we hold. These occurrences form as the building blocks for our stories. Think about it. Would you want a story written about you that was made of all of the building blocks of your not-so-finer moments in life? You know, the moments when you weren't so gentle. The moments when you lost your composure and self-restraint. I think not. That would be a story to be more ashamed of than proud. Please repeat after me. "I am a gentle communicator."

Chapter 14:
I Am Patient

Ingredient #9

Have you ever lashed out at someone only to find out later that the person was going through hard times? We all have, and when we do, we feel like absolute schmucks. So, the story's moral is that we need to be better at being patient in three key areas: one with ourselves, two with situations, and lastly, with others.

Have you ever heard of being emotionally mature? How about being spiritually mature? If you haven't, let's give you a quick lesson on each. Emotional maturity is all about not boomeranging the energy of another back at them. A good example is when another motorist flips you off because you unintentionally cut in front of them. This is a prime example of emotional immaturity. This emotionally immature person is simply absorbing the energy from a weak moment and allowing it to dictate their actions in the present. Does someone cutting you off warrant the middle finger? If you are emotionally immature, it does. However, it certainly does not if you are mature, disciplined, and full of love and grace.

To make matters worse, most people get into a spitting match of dysfunctional and undisciplined energy. One finger rises and then another. Soon, you find yourself in a battle of road rage. This scenario is one where the admirable and attractive quality of patience is nowhere to be found.

Now, take the concept of spiritual maturity; when individuals are spiritually mature, they recognize that incredible energy is at play, and at times, it's downright dark. Those who are spiritually mature understand that there is a dark force out there that looks to exploit the weakness within us all to provoke us into confrontation. Why? Because when we are duped into confrontation with the wrongly perceived enemy, it leads to division and isolation. It makes us lonelier. A grand plan is at play that's devious and destructive at best.

So, what's the ideal course of action? It's to combine the superpowers of being emotionally and spiritually mature to enable you to fly high above the fray. Yes, we have mentioned that ingredient previously. They go hand in hand and are the secret sauce when combined. Let's explore the following three scenarios: patience with ourselves, circumstance, and others.

Patience with ourselves - Ask anyone to describe the five top things they struggle with, and I guarantee patience is in their top five. Also, hitting the top five would be consistency. All humans struggle with consistency. The only place they don't have a problem being consistent is when they are being hard on themselves. Can I get an "Amen" to that? Yup, you are nodding your head right now in affirmation. Why? Because our internal voice won't give us a break. If it's not condemning us, it's pushing us to do more and more. It's constantly whispering, "You haven't done enough." We need to stop listening to this internal critic. We need to give ourselves a break. We must be patient with ourselves, accomplish what we can, and then sit in peace, knowing that we are giving life our best. Doesn't that sound peaceful? If that narrative is attractive, it's because it was meant to be. That narrative is the epitome of internal patience.

Patience for circumstance - Do you ever feel like life is attacking from all angles? If so, you are not alone. I warn my coaching clients when they start coaching with me, that the dark side, which I have mentioned, is sure to attack from every direction. Why? Because what God and I do for folks via coaching is to restore them to their most vital energy. This is the exact opposite of what the dark side desires. How will they be attacked? One, through their internal narratives, that critical voice. Two, from the weakness within other people. And lastly, via circumstance. Have you ever said this to yourself? "I just can't catch a break!" or "When it rains, it pours." These are all sayings reflective of being attacked. These are also instances where people claim to be unaware. A lack of awareness and accountability leads to a victim state. This is incredibly dangerous. Why? Because you might as well be signaling for the universe to beat on you some more.

Circumstance is a favorite tool of the dark side. Why? Because it's a great tool to coax you into a compromised state. Because with circumstance also comes no clear person to blame. It's just happening, and most think it's coincidental. You know how I feel about coincidence. Nope, I don't believe in it. Everything is connected. So how do we combat circumstance? Patience is the answer. How many times have you run into a circumstance and proclaimed, in an instant, it's a bad thing? I bet all the time. How many times have you declared a circumstance as unchangeable? I bet many times. Why do we do this? Because our vision, when it comes to the road ahead, is limited at best. How often have things turned out okay and even better in the long run? I don't know about you, but it always happens to me. It's as if we all need to say, "Wait for it. Wait for it." Why? Because patience is sure to lead you to a more significant result. Have patience for circumstance because today's circumstance rarely defines your everlasting destination.

Patience with others - This is the biggie. Why? Because people rock us off our center a lot. I don't know about you, but I lose my patience and do it often with people. I like to think that I am more emotionally and spiritually mature than that, but perhaps I'm not. From time to time, people push my buttons. Why is patience key when others are poking at the proverbial bear? Because rarely do people come at you with the real problem. Instead, the issue is just a surface indicator of a deeper problem. Take the following instance, for example. A woman walks into a management office for an apartment community. She is having one of those days and is about to let it go on a management company representative. Why is she about to lose her collective shizzle? Because her toilet is backed up, and crap is everywhere. It sounds pretty urgent, but does it sound like something that warrants abusing a management staff member? I think not. More often than not, if someone goes on the attack, it's because they are being attacked themselves. This is where patience enters the picture. The staff member must have the patience, empathy, and discipline to move into "care mode" rather than "attack mode" in return. They must possess the emotional maturity and fortitude that allows them to maintain a higher and more vital position than the circumstance being presented to them. They must know that something greater is afoot at a spiritual level. Who knows what that woman had encountered up until the point when she walked into the rental office? Perhaps her three teenagers mentally abused her before her toilet backed up. Maybe she had fought with her husband that morning. Who knows, she might have received a call from her Mother telling her that her Mom was dying of cancer. If any of these things had occurred, it would be cause for grace and understanding. We must have patience for others in the moment as we have no idea what the previous moments represent.

Chapter 15:
I Am Grateful

Ingredient #10

What exactly is gratitude? If you believe in the law of attraction as I do, it's simply a frequency of abundance. Have you ever heard the saying, "If you give, you too shall receive?" If so, it's the essence of the law of attraction. Simply put, it's a philosophy that entails a boomerang of your energy. What you lead with is sure to follow. You are the magnet, and nothing, I mean nothing, is attracted to you by happenstance. In a nutshell, leading with a frequency of gratitude is a surefire way to manifest even greater abundance.

But let's be honest. The truth is, it's hard sometimes to remain centered in gratitude; regardless of what is going on in your life. I know. Take it from me, as I am an expert in harnessing the power of the law of attraction. It's a choice you must make daily. For some of us, it might be an all-out brawl to land on a platform of gratitude. Every day, I challenge coaching clients to rewrite their negative and defeating narratives. Why? Because their very future depends upon their ability to write powerfully. I suppose you could call me a spin doctor, because I believe there's a silver lining in every situation.

People need to look hard enough. Take, for instance, the institution of marriage. If you are in the thick of things regarding a dysfunctional marriage, it's most likely super challenging to write an empowering story about marriage and a grateful one. However, the silver lining can be found if you only take the time to look hard enough. Are there children in the marriage? If so, the silver lining can be your children. Think about it. If you have three kids, then your husband or wife is responsible for giving you three of the greatest gifts on the planet, and your blessing compounds with every day. Here's another scenario. Let's assume you are in a season full of trials and tribulations. You eventually bust out of the season and have gained great admiration for your perseverance. You have forged greater character by not just surviving but also through thriving. Perhaps you have learned valuable life lessons along the way. Maybe you have taught your kids to roll with the punches and come out on top. Perhaps you have taught them that it's more admirable to dig in than flee from a difficult situation. Perhaps you have saved them from a divorce in the future. If so, it's your choice. Do you choose to focus on the trial, tribulation, or silver lining of abundance? You must choose gratitude. Why? Because celebrated gratitude in your life is directly proportional to the amount of joy you experience in life.

Chapter 16:
I Find the Joy

Ingredient #11

You have two choices. Find joy or swim around in something less. Sounds like a no-brainer decision. More or less, you choose. Why choose more? There are so many reasons. Nobody likes to be around an Eeyore. Do you remember that donkey in Winnie the Pooh? He was always walking around proclaiming that the sky was falling. He was hard to watch as his pessimism and doom and gloom seemed to be contagious. It was sure to bring you down. This holds true for people in life. Nobody wants to hang with those who tow the cloud around. Life is hard enough as it is. Very rarely do you see people flocking to those who celebrate a problem. Instead, they usually run in the opposite direction.

Joy is a choice. It's attractive. But it's also a healthy way to live. Do you recall when I recited all the adverse health effects of being lonely? Well, the opposite of that cocktail for an early grave holds for those who choose to live a joyous existence. There's less stress, and the anxiety drifts away. Those who are joyful are out, about, and active. Therefore, their bodies are more robust. Studies show that people tend to live longer when joy is a fixture. Do you need any more convincing as to which choice to make?

Is it simply a choice to be grateful and ultimately joyful? The choice, without a doubt, is at least half the battle. The other half is staying committed to accentuating the joy in your life. Are you committed to highlighting the joy? Yes, we can take three practical steps to ensure that the joy is present and accounted for in our lives. They are as follows:

Be laser-focused.

Every morning, as we wake, we must be on a mission to find joy! I find joy! Be laser-focused. You may need a teacher. If so, watch a child. They are the inventors of joy unless they are spitting up pea soup. Yes, children seem to have a range of emotions, but when joyful, they don't hold back. They explode into joy. They are giggling, dancing, singing, and twirling around for no reason. Why are children so free to experience joy? Because they are uncluttered. Do you recall when I was talking about the power of your story? The same holds true for joy. Your story must be open to it, so much so that you can receive it. If your vessel is cluttered with deficient or less-than-joyful stories, joy can't flow through you. Children are the most fantastic example of a free-flowing vessel. They have no clutter. They have no disempowering stories. Therefore, joy flows through them like a fire hose. Watch them. Learn from them. It's a contagion, but in a good way. Find the joy! Be the firehose!

Don't kick it down the street.

We are constantly moving the goalpost. The problem is when we move the goalpost, we also delay the potential for joy. Are you one of those people who sets a goal, accomplishes it, celebrates for about sixty seconds, and then sets another goal? Do you see the lunacy in what you are doing? You are constantly chasing joy rather than enjoying and or celebrating it. Enjoy it. Yeah, that's right. We need to sink into and be present with joy. Roll around in it. Bask in it. Bathe in it. Allow it to swallow us whole so those around us have trouble telling where the joy in us begins or ends. Do you see all the ingredients of the secret sauce weaving themselves together? We need to be present in the moment with joy. We must accentuate the positive and find as much joy daily as possible. Have you ever asked someone how their day is going, and they respond with, "I'm just happy to be breathing!" This epitomizes launching out of the gate with gratitude and joy. When we accentuate the small, joyous things, our life has no choice but to get bigger and even more amazing.

Celebrate and broadcast it.

Have you ever heard someone say, "Don't be boastful." Well, this does not apply to joy. We must boast about the joy in our lives. We must celebrate it whenever we can. Why? Because celebrating joy is also the act of broadcasting our gratitude. When we are grateful, the universe must send us more. Why? Because we are good stewards of the joy. It's not wasted on us. Have you ever seen or heard someone downplaying the joy in their lives? I bet you have. It's almost as though they are afraid that the shoe is about to drop. News flash! You can either promote the shoe or the joy, you choose. I choose the joy!

Chapter 17:
I Love Big in Small Ways

Ingredient #12

Have you noticed? There are no pictures in this book but one, this one.

Allow me to introduce you to my guardian angels. Rodney and Phyllis Mott. These are my parents in the prime of their lives. Yes, they had just married, and my three siblings and I were but a sparkle in their eyes. They have since passed. My Mom passed long ago from pancreatic cancer, and my father crossed over from natural causes shortly before the pandemic.

Notice I didn't say, "I lost my parents." This is one of my least favorite phrases. Why? Because if you understand the nature of life and the aging process, if you subscribe to the notion that you "lose" people, you are destined to become a bigger and bigger loser as you travel down life's highway. My use of the word "pass" was intentional because I believe that when our loved ones pass, they take a higher seat in the bleachers of the universe. Yes, they are promoted to guardian angel status. My narrative consists of one where I can chat with my Dad and Mom anytime. I can call on them for guidance and strength. Most importantly, I feel their love daily and pick up on signs from them just saying a gentle hello via people and circumstances. Isn't that a more empowering and comforting narrative than "I lost my parents?"

Get ready for this statement, as you may not like it. We are destined to become the good, bad, and ugly of precisely who our parents are or were. Yes, depending on what kind of people your parents are or were, you're most likely cringing right now. It's true. The generational curse is a real thing. It's a gravitational pull like no other on the planet. Modeled behavior and energy passed on from parent to child is a grooming force. It guides people into engaging in destructive acts even though their rational minds know it's wrong. How do we break the generational curse? The answer is comprised of two words: vigilance and commitment. We must be aware of all the characteristics our parents pass along to us. We need to be hyper-aware of their modeling bad and ugly traits. Then, we need to be super convicted via sustained commitment when establishing traits and behavioral patterns contrary to those weaker patterns. We must develop and cement stronger patterns or rhythms in their wake.

Who was my father, and what was his greatest lesson? Often, I think when I write, God whispers to me. He puts notions in my head which I have a hard time believing are mine alone. He often coaches me through my coaching with others. This morning and this notion is one of those times. Rodney Mott. Who was he? He was a great Dad. Was he perfect? No way close, but even in his imperfection, he was made perfect for me. There He goes again. "Even in his imperfection, he was made perfect for me." Those are not my words! Those words are too good to be mine. You may want to marinate on those a bit. You might want to reflect upon all the imperfect people in your life and how they were made perfect for you, even in their imperfections.

The truth is, I have struggled in the past with my father's imperfections. If I'm a hundred percent honest with you, I have resented my father for his imperfections from time to time, as they have caused me pain and suffering. One is because I have had to watch them on display while causing carnage in the lives of others. And two, because I have followed in his dysfunctional footsteps more than once. There's that generational curse in full force. God is knocking hard on my door right now. He is saying it's time to let go, Chris. It's time to forgive and forgive again. It's time to hold onto the good.

Believe me. At this moment, I am having a defining moment! This notion is bringing tears to my eyes. Sap alert! I was speaking in Vegas, and when I got to this topic, I had to push back the tears when talking about my Dad. We shed tears more easily in our older and perhaps wiser years. Why is that? Maybe it's because things matter more. Perhaps it's because we understand they should matter more and that moments and time are precious. Perhaps we see the end of the road for ourselves and know we only have limited time.

My father was perfect for me. He was funny. He was a loving man. He liked to be the center of attention. Shocker. Where did I get that from? Apple, tree, as they say. He was creative. He was a master Gardner and liked to create things. I am all those things, and for that, I am so grateful.

But what was his greatest lesson? There are so many. But first, a little back story. As my father grew older, I moved him from California to Colorado to be closer to us. I remember picking him up to take him out of the assisted living facility every week. Needless to say, because of his age, he had trouble getting into my Toyota Tundra. So I would grab his right ass cheek to lift him into the truck. I told him, "Dad, whenever I grab your ass, I want you to tell me to get my hand off your ass." So he did. But he added a twist to it, as he always did. He'd say, "Get your hand off my ass!" But then he would give me an exaggerated wink! Hold onto this, as it's super important later in the story. Fast forward to his passing. Dad started declining, so we brought him home for hospice care at the doctor's advice.

Little did I know this would serve as the stage for my Dad's most significant lesson or gift to me. I had already been through my

Mom's passing, so she had set the standard for memorials. Multitudes of people from all over the country had descended upon California to pay their respects and show their love for my Mom. Why? Because my Mom was selfless. She was a lifelong giver and created a huge impact. So, my greatest fear was that because of my father's selfish nature, there wouldn't be many to say their last goodbyes or pay their respects. There was no funeral or memorial for my father. The hospital bed was sitting in the corner of my living room. But this was to be the grandest of stages. This was the venue for his greatest lesson. All my father's life, he had taught me to count. He taught me to count the physical things, which he possessed. He taught me to count credit cards and credit limits. These were not the finest of lessons. But in his final act, he taught me to stop counting. The reality was that as he was experiencing his last moments with us, it wasn't about the quantity of people who surrounded him, but rather, the quality. Fifteen or twenty of the most that mattered were all there. It was perfect. Again, imperfectly perfect. And when he was done teaching me that final lesson, he didn't have the strength to utter a single word. He simply and so profoundly gave me one exaggerated wink as he was holding my hand. He then took his final breath. Thank you Dad for all that you were and weren't because together, it formed the perfect role model.

Who was my mother, and what was her greatest lesson? Now for the final ingredient in the secret sauce. Love big in small ways. Don't take the cookies!!! Ok, now you have lost it, Mott. What the heck are you talking about? I am talking about the cookies! Whenever corporate profits decline, what they decide to cut from operational budgets always baffles me. The cookies are the first to go. They should be last. Why? Because they genuinely are the most minor expenditure that garner the greatest return. How so? Because proverbial warm-baked cookies become the highlight of any industry. People will make it a point to visit just for a cookie. I know it. It seems silly, but it's more strategic than anything. In the apartment industry, we had our residents trained to salivate when they saw us. We had them conditioned to know that we were givers. We had them trained to understand that cookies come with fellowship. On a subliminal front, they knew that we represented community and the cure to loneliness, and we did it all with a single cookie. We loved big in small ways.

My mother was the essence of this notion. She was the Director of Nursing at Children's Hospital at Stanford University. She was a lifelong caregiver. She was very dedicated to her profession but also very wacky and rarely took herself too seriously. Again, apple, tree, I had no chance but to become her. I can remember the memorial service as though it was yesterday. This lady got up to speak about my Mom and told a story about replacing my Mom in her capacity at Children's Hospital. She explained how nervous she was when replacing my Mom and filling her enormous shoes. She then mentioned that her nerves were calmed by the notion that she could train with my Mom for a few weeks. However, as the days passed, she became increasingly nervous because my Mom only taught her where the ribbon was in her top drawer, where the balloons were in her bottom drawer, and finally, where the helium was in her closet. When she uttered these words, the crowd cried and laughed simultaneously. Why? Because they all knew that this was the essence of my Mom. Mom was all about loving big in small ways. At every opportunity, she would champion your story and celebrate you. She was super present in the moment. She found joy every day. She showed her gratitude for others by attaching balloons to your chair, office door, or even your hair to draw attention to each individual's uniqueness. She was the essence of the secret sauce, so people couldn't even conceptualize not being there to send her off and pay their love and respect for her. My mom's greatest gift and lesson (to me and everyone she touched) was Love BIG in small but MIGHTY ways. Thanks Mom:-))))

Chapter 18: Your Eulogy

The owner of Sherpa Real Estate recently held an off-site meeting to give us perspective on the year we just traveled and set our perspective for the year to come. He conducted a super powerful exercise with us at the end of this mini-retreat. He started by stating that the average lifespan of an American these days is 77.28 years. He said that if you had someone in your family who lived longer than this age, you could add 3.5 years. In my case, my Grandmother lived to the ripe old age of 102. Therefore, I was to add to the average lifespan. Then he said if you had someone who passed earlier than that number due to some heredity disease, you needed to subtract 3.5 years. There went my additional years because my Mom passed at 69 from pancreatic cancer. The two numbers canceled themselves out, and now I was left with 77.28 years. He then instructed us to subtract our current age from that number. Subtract 55 from 77.28, and you're left with...

22.28 years

I singled out that number and put it in bold on purpose. Why? Because I want you to marinate on it for just a bit. I want you to contemplate what that number means. I sure did. It represents just over two decades of opportunity left. It means that my window of life is shrinking. And if you prescribe to the notion that "Tomorrow is never a guarantee," well, let's just say it's a sobering cup of perspective at best. This point of introspection was precisely what Chris Liverett, the owner of Sherpa Real Estate, was attempting to accomplish. He wanted to wake us up, not so much from a professional perspective, but rather, a personal one.

Once he allowed that number to sink in, he gave us one not-so-simple direction. "Now, I want you to write your eulogy." I want you to fast forward to your memorial and tell us what you hope and desire that others will say about you when you are gone. What a powerful and exciting exercise. The ultimate point of this exercise was to shed light upon who we are today and who we need to become for that wish of a eulogy to become a reality. It was intended to illuminate where we might be missing the mark and give us the power of enlightenment to change course. He gave us fifteen minutes to complete this exercise with the caveat that it would need to be a work in progress. Why? Because this is your legacy, we are talking about. Your legacy deserves reflection upon the relationships, which you have nurtured in life. It deserves care. It deserves positive reflection. It deserves flying high to write the best possible outcome. It deserves forgiving and holding onto just the good. It deserves you to be present, seizing the most significant moments of your time. It deserves a gentle pen. It deserves patience. It deserves a good dose of both your gratitude and joyful muscle. And most important, it deserves the highlight real of all who have loved you and who you have loved in small but significant ways. Did you catch what I did? I intentionally just added all the secret sauce ingredients into your eulogy. Why? Because it's the surefire way to place your stamp on the hearts and souls of others.

Because I am a writer and do these reflective exercises with my coaching clients daily, I was able to whip my first draft of my eulogy out super quick. For this book, however, I have taken some time and tailored a eulogy using the twelve ingredients mentioned above. So please sit back and take this Eulogy in; take it in as though it was yours.

Your Eulogy

"I lived a powerful story. I was a community builder and embraced that awesome responsibility. I was loved by many, for being a champion of others. I was a masterful atmosphere architect who created a trusted space where deep relationships flourish. I held the keys to the cure for loneliness. I was a healer by creating an inclusive and caring place to work and live. I was gentle and patient and made others feel a sense of belonging. I flew high above the fray and always walked in the strength of joy and gratitude. I will be remembered for loving BIG in small ways."

The operative question is, was it enough? Would this eulogy do justice to the opportunity that life represents? If your answer is a resounding "yes," so be it. If not, we must write it repeatedly until it becomes super powerful. We need to revise it until tears come to your eyes. A life well spent is one worthy of shedding tears over.

Chapter 19:
You Are the Secret Sauce

Ever watch football? If so, you know the term "the head fake." For those who don't watch football, it's simply a term for when the Quarterback fakes out the defensive players by looking in one direction with his eyes but then throws the ball in a different direction. This entire time, I have been engaging in one big head fake. I really couldn't give a rat's behind about who you are professionally. Yes, there's value in the workplace, as we spend much of our lives at our jobs. But what I am really after is your soul and spirit. I have been engaging in one big head fake to coax you into a better state of being. I am after who you are and who you can become as a human being. Why? Because if you adopt the twelve ingredients of The Generational Sauce, the planet is bound to be a better place.

www.ingramcontent.com/pod-product-compliance
Lightning Source LLC
Chambersburg PA
CBHW071948210526
45479CB00003B/859